Our Family Adventures

by
Melanie Antonia

Our Family Adventures

Copyright © by Author: Melanie Antonia, 2024

Cover Illustration by: Dylan Fernandez

The right of Melanie Antonia to be identified legally as Author of this work has been asserted in accordance with sections 77 and 78 of the Copyright, Designs and Patents Act, 1988.

Published by: Melanie Antonia Fernandez, London, 2024
With the service of: TamaRe House, UK
044 (0) 844 357 2592, www.tamarehouse.com

ISBN: 978-1-7395513-2-2

All rights are reserved. No part of this book may be reprinted, copied or stored in retrieval systems of any type, except by written permission from the Author or Publishers. Parts of this book may, however, be used only on reference to support related documents or subjects.

This publication uses archival-quality paper

A CIP record of this publication is available from the British Library.

Our Family Adventures

Contents

Acknowledgments 5
Our First Christmas with Ellie 6
Our Picnic Adventure 9
Our visit to the Pet Shop 12
The Fun Fair 15
Ellie and Mum walk 10,000 steps daily 19

Acknowledgments

This book is written and dedicated to my children, Shane, Dylan and Ellie.

Without them, life would never have challenged me to step out of my comfort zone and reach for what I thought was impossible.

Never stop believing in your ability to be great and shine in a world that can sometimes shadow us. Be bold, confident and step out.

I will always be your biggest fan!

Mum x

I love you

Our First Christmas with Ellie

♥♥♥

Christmas time was always an exciting time of year for the family. The front room would get all jazzed up with shimmering decorations, twinkly lights and quirky, musical, toys that mum collected over the years. Mum loved adding at least one new item to the Christmas collection. The windows would get a make-over with stick on snowflakes and icicle lights, that would drape across the centre.

Mum, as a child, had fond memories of walking around her local streets at Christmas time, where she would look and admire the Christmas spirit, that everyone embraced in their front gardens and windows. The more extravagant the better. Especially the houses that had ornaments lit up on the roof tops. Mum was in awe. Every year she would remind Shane and Dylan of the sleigh that used to drive down her road as a child. It was supported by a local church charity. The Santa lookalike would sit on his sleigh, hoisted on a truck, with cut out wooden reindeers and flashing colourful lights and shout 'Merry Christmas', to the adults and children, as they stood in their front gardens. The children would wave excitedly, whilst the adults placed a small donation, for the collectors of the charity in their tin cans. It was a joyous time for mum and her family and brought their local community closer.

Shane and Dylan, as they got older had the task of setting up the 6ft Christmas tree. It was a pre-lit bargain, as mum would say, but the boys would still add extra lights to give it the wow factor. This year, however, Christmas was going to be extra special. It was going to be their little sister Ellie's, first Christmas! Instead of two stockings, there were now three, Ellie's was smaller, (for now), with a sequined unicorn sewn on the front. She wasn't really at the age where she was going to demand anything bigger than a teether or rattle, mum joked, as she placed Ellie's in the middle of Shane and Dylan's.

Whilst mum, Shane and Dylan were decorating the front room, Ellie was enjoying her afternoon nap. The boys were desperate for her to wake up! It wasn't long after that Ellie was babbling and giggling away to herself in her cot. The boys leapt off the sofa and dashed straight into her room!! Shane carefully picked her up and gave her cuddles and Dylan softly brushed back her hair away from her face. They tiptoed to the front room door, counted "1, 2 3" and then opened the door slowly. The reflection of the twinkling lights started to fall on their faces, Ellie's smile got bigger, and she started to stretch out her hands and clasp them in and out. This was her way of asking for something. Shane walked her over to the tree, whilst Dylan handed over the Angelic star, that traditionally had sat at the top. He handed it to Ellie and Shane raised her higher. Mum was ready to capture the moment on her phone. Shane, Dylan and Ellie all held a part of the star Angel and placed it together at the top of the tree. Now, Christmas season in their home, was ready to commence.

Our Picnic Adventure

It was the hottest day of the summer so far. Shane, Dylan and Ellie decided to go for a picnic. Mum was at work, so together they packed a delicious, healthy and refreshing lunch.

In their basket were fruit salad pots, mixed with strawberries, apples, kiwi, grapes and mango, pineapple jam sandwiches, cheesy crisps (Ellie's favourite) and bottles of iced water!

Off they went, Ellie in the middle, as she was the youngest. Shane and Dylan would often hold one hand each, count to three and then swing her high in the air. As her feet lifted swiftly off the ground, she would giggle so much! They would use this as a way of stopping her little legs from getting tired, from the walking.

Walking through the woods to get to the park, was always exciting. They never knew who or what they would come across and today was no exception. The most elegant, red-breasted Robin was perched on a branch. The branch just skimmed the top of Shane and Dylan's heads, as they passed by. As they looked back at the Robin, they noticed its body turned, in the direction that they were walking and tweeted softly, as if it was saying goodbye.

They arrived at the park. Shane and Dylan opened up the picnic blanket and Ellie started to lay out their food. She was so excited and loved spending time with her big brothers. The boys were very protective over their little sister and mum found much happiness in the bond that they had as siblings.

The grass was a glorious green and shimmered when the sunlight caught the tips. As they ate all the yummy snacks they prepared, they took it in turns to play 'I Spy'. Ellie would always spy that she saw an animal, that you would more than likely find in the zoo or even the wild, but the boys loved her so much that they went along with the game and pretended that they could see, whatever animal or object Ellie imagined.

It was time to rest and enjoy their iced water. Refreshed and cooled down it was time to lay down in the relaxing sun.

Ellie put her sun-cream on after, her brothers did theirs, as she would copy. Mum always said to them, that the best way to teach their little sister, would be lead as an example – she was right. Ellie learnt so much independence spending time with her brothers and this made it easier for her when she had to settle into nursery and school.

After some time, they got up and packed away their wrappers and headed back through the woods and arrived home.

As they opened the front door, mum greeted them in the kitchen. She served them a treat, with a bowl of two scoops of their favourite vanilla ice-cream, with lots of sprinkles!

"This was the best picnic day ever!", Ellie shrieked, and everyone laughed together.

Our visit to the Pet Shop

It took over a year, but they did it! Shane, Dylan and Ellie had saved all their pocket money in a jar, for this very special day.

The day had finally arrived, when mum was taking them to the pet shop!! They were all very excited and woke up, before daylight even started to peek through their bedroom window.

It was a special day for their family. They ate their breakfast so fast, that it was mum left at the table, still sipping her hot coffee! They rushed to bathroom and helped each other get ready for their memorable day.

Belts on and there were smiles all around. Ellie carried her toy puppy, Ralphy, in her backpack. She told her brothers that Ralphy needed to be happy as well. The boys did everything they could to make Ellie happy and agreed that Ralphy had to be happy too.

Mum knew how much they desperately wanted a puppy and was proud of them all, for working together to save their money. It was a dream come true for all of them and they had to wait so patiently whilst they saved.

When they arrived at the pet shop, they looked around at the tropical fish. It was fascinating to watch the fish blowing bubbles to the top of the water. You couldn't help but watch and copy them as they put their lips together and opened their mouths to breathe.

Rabbits were darting around their hutches with excitement, seeing children running up and down. Chinchillas gnawing on soft wood, completely unaware of anyone else around them.

Finally, mum, Shane, Dylan and Ellie made their way to the puppy section. Mum kept "awing", at all of them and Shane and Dylan would just look at each other a shake their heads and laugh.

Among the Beagles, Labradors, Golden retrievers and Bichon Frise puppies in the shop, Shane, Dylan and Ellie fell in love straight away with the Boarder Collie. He was curled up in the corner of the pen. As soon as they saw him, they all agreed that this little puppy would be going home with them. Mum was given the honour of naming him. She decided to call him Tyler.

Shane, Dylan and Ellie counted out from their pocket money a total of £320. Mum doubled checked it for them, and handed the money to the pet shop owner. Mum decided whilst they were there, she would buy their new family member, Tyler, some treats. She bought a personalised collar, food bowl, water bowl and even a winter jacket.

The car journey home was full of smiles, happiness and lots of cuddles with their new puppy! And of course, Ralphy was very happy with their choice.

The Fun Fair

The alarm had gone off! The sun was beaming! It was the first day of the half term. Shane and Dylan rushed into Ellie's room. She was already awake with excitement, packing her bag for the day ahead.

Mum was taking them to the local fun fair! Even though they had saved up their pocket money, mum had envelopes ready on the kitchen table, each with their names on them, next to a bottle of homemade lemonade, perfect for the warm day.

Mum worked long hours and always felt so guilty that she couldn't spend much time with her children during the holidays, but when she could, she made sure they had the best times together.

Today they decided instead of taking the car, they were going to get the bus and then walk a short distance to the fun fair. Caps on, sunglasses and spending money in their pockets. Tyler was joining the family on their day out too. They were ready to set out to the bus stop. Ellie and mum held the lead together.

As they waited at the bus stop, Izzy and Jake, who lived a few doors down, joined them. Tyler was jumping with joy. He remembered them, as they would stop by the front garden and play with him. They were going to the fun fair as well. A few moments later the bus arrived.

The journey on the bus took around forty minutes but went by so quickly. Time spent chatting and sharing jokes with each other, always meant time flew by.

As they approached the park, the music roaring from the rides and children playing and having fun could be heard. Everyone was so excited! Wrist bands sorted and tied on, they were ready to go and have fun!

Tyler was in his element. As soon as he entered the fair, he could smell delicious hot dogs, burgers and onions cooking. It was going to be heaven! Remnant pieces of food lay await for him to scoop with his mouth, as mum and Ellie walked along with him.

First ride was bumper cars; Shane was first to sit with Ellie as she couldn't reach the pedals but was able to steer the car well. She had practise from her steering wheel, that she was given as a Christmas present. It was a beautiful soft pink and made real life car noises. Ellie would often take her steering wheel in the car.

When Ellie and mum went food shopping, mum would call out to Ellie, "now we are turning left", and Ellie would press the left indicator button and turn the steering wheel.

They had so much fun chasing Dylan around the pit area. Now it was time to change over and Ellie's turn to Chase Shane. Dylan fastened Ellie in and ready, steady, go! They were off at top speed. Shane already knew Ellie's moves, but he allowed her to catch him a few times at least.

The pony express was next on the list. Shane and Dylan took Tyler for a walk whilst mum and Ellie went on the pony ride together. It was so relaxing. You could faintly hear the tiny gallops from the pony and feel the breeze as it graced their faces whilst they moved around the circuit.

Mum climbed off first and stretched her arms out to Ellie, gently pulled her down and gave her the biggest of hugs and whispered, "love you pickle pop". Ellie giggled and repeated "pickle pop, pickle pop", as she skipped along with mum, to find her brothers and Tyler.

Shane and Dylan enjoyed the more adventurous and daring rides like the reverse bungee, twister, helter-skelter and house of terror. Whilst Ellie and mum took delight in the teacup ride and luxury carousel. Ellie and mum felt like exquisite royalty as they twirled around on the golden carriages.

Before they set off to make their way home, Shane, Dylan, Ellie and Mum, decided to treat themselves to a bag of cotton candy and a mouth-watering iced slush. Mum had packed extra special 'dog friendly' treats for Tyler so he wouldn't feel left out.

Ellie had so much fun and was exhausted!! She fell asleep almost straight away, on the bus journey home. Shane and Dylan took it in turns to carry her back safely, making sure not to wake her. Mum cradled Tyler in her arms. He never knew being part of this new family could bring so much happiness. Later that evening they all sat down to watch a family film, with some homemade sweet popcorn. A relaxing evening to the perfect day.

Ellie and Mum walk 10,000 steps daily

Ellie had just turned six months old and was very inquisitive about the environment around her. Mum decided she was going to sign up and step up to the challenge of walking 10,000 daily. This was the charity challenge of the month. Mum was very passionate about raising money or fundraising for charities. She knew too many friends and family affected, in some way or another. Sadly, some of her closet friends died and went to heaven. Mum ordered her and Ellie matching t-shits. She was filled excitement when arrived.

Day one was upon them, and the weather offered, was a glorious day of sun light combined with a gentle breeze. The breeze was a God send, as later took the edge off for mum. All the fast past walking, generated, mastering pushing the buggy up steeper slopes – the cool breeze made the uphill battle more bearable.

For mum this was a luxury, as she usually drove everywhere, Now, she combined spending time with her newborn daughter, exploring hidden gems, all whilst raising money for charity. They spent days observing the radiant daffodils in bloom, that lay beautifully in local gardens and churches. Taking breaks in coffee shops, sitting on benches watching the tranquil swans swim up and down the lake. They dipped their heads from time to time in the water, as a way of refreshing their soft, white, silky coats. Squirrels would entertain Ellie by dashing over to collect an acorn and then scoot back up the tree to enjoy a good gnaw! Day 19 of the walk was extra special, it was Mother's Day. Dylan had booked a table at an Italian restaurant mum admired for years. She would often say to the boys, one day we will eat there. The boys never really gave it much thought until they got older. They realised that the restaurant mum referred to over the years, was quite expensive. Now, Dylan had a part time job and Shane had worked the previous summer. They decided to put some money aside and as a way of showing appreciation to their mum, they planned a surprise. Dylan told mum that she needed to get Ellie and herself ready for 7:30pm and not to eat dinner! Mum was excited but also nervous as to what they had arranged. When the cab came to pick them up, the driver assisted mum with the buggy, whilst Dylan and Shane helped Ellie in her car seat. As they approached the restaurant, mum had tears in her eyes and glanced over to Dylan. He smiled and told her that she deserved to be treated to something special, after all she had sacrificed over the years. The meal was spectacular and beyond mum's expectations. The evening was filled with laughter, reminiscing and of course ended with a luscious trio of deserts each! Ellie had taken so much sensory that she fell asleep peacefully. For the remaining days of the walk, it was spent exploring local parks, grabbing a bargain in the local shops and circuit walking.

Ellie and mum achieved a total of 352,009 steps!

www.ingramcontent.com/pod-product-compliance
Lightning Source LLC
Chambersburg PA
CBHW042321090526
44585CB00024BA/2784